636.088   Ross, Michael Elsohn,
ROS   1952-

Indoor zoo.

W9-BJK-203

$23.93   34880030001809

DATE			
4			

INDOOR ZOO

Michael Elsohn Ross

with illustrations by Tim Seeley

🌿 Carolrhoda Books, Inc./Minneapolis

To Ginny and her menagerie
—M.E.R.

To Mike and Marlene (the 'rents)
—T.S.

Text copyright © 2003 by Michael Elsohn Ross
Illustrations copyright © 2003 by Carolrhoda Books, Inc.

Carolrhoda Books, Inc.
A division of Lerner Publishing Group
241 First Avenue North, Minneapolis, MN 55401 U.S.A.

Website address: www.lernerbooks.com

Library of Congress Cataloging-in-Publication Data

Ross, Michael Elsohn, 1952–
    Indoor zoo / by Michael Elsohn Ross ; illustrations by Tim Seeley.
    p.   cm. — (You are the scientist)
    Includes index.
    Summary: Explores the animals that live in our homes, from dogs to cats to ladybugs and houseflies.
    ISBN: 0–87614–621–3 (lib. bdg. : alk. paper)
    1. Pets—Miscellanea—Juvenile literature.
2. Household animals—Miscellanea—Juvenile literature. 3. Science—Experiments—Juvenile literature. [1. Pets. 2. Household animals.]
I. Seeley, Tim, ill. II. Title.
SF416.2 .R66 2003
636.088'7—dc21   2001006134

Manufactured in the United States of America
1 2 3 4 5 6 – JR – 08 07 06 05 04 03

TABLE OF CONTENTS

THE ZOO AT HOME

Imagine working at a zoo. All day long, you could be with animals. You could play with snakes and dive with the dolphins. You could watch the tigers and the polar bears to discover what makes them tick.

Sometimes you may feel like your house is a zoo, but have you ever realized that it may truly be one? In addition to any younger siblings, dogs, and cats that live there, your home is host to a whole crew of uninvited guests. Some, such as dust mites, are too small to see. Others, such as houseflies, may be too hard to ignore.

When you were a little kid, you began to learn about the world by playing with everything around you. You became a scientist at play. Whether you play with Lego blocks, puppies, broken VCRs, or soggy cereal, you end up using a variety of science skills. You observe, question, test, predict, solve problems, and invent. It's easy to forget that science can be playful, but science is a good excuse for playing, and playing is a great way to explore!

YOUR LABORATORY

To start on a zoological expedition doesn't require a lot of expensive gear or a large party of explorers. All it takes is paying attention to the other living creatures around you. Here are a few tips:

► Be gentle with animals both large and small. There is no need to hurt creatures that you want to learn about.

► **Forget about** any tests with dangerous substances.

► When you have an experiment in progress, alert other members of your household. Perhaps you can make a sign that states there is an important animal experiment in action!

► To let your local adults know that studying household critters is worthwhile, show them the following article from the fictional magazine column "Popular Scientists":

SPIDER WISDOM

by Eric Nid

Sparta, New Jersey "My parents thought I was crazy when I started studying our household spiders instead of shooing them out the door. I knew they weren't dangerous. And I liked them even though my folks didn't," stated the world famous biologist, Humberto Cruz, at his lakeside laboratory. Cruz learned that his spiders ate lots of pesky flies. He started counting the number snagged each week. His parents were impressed by his results and supported him in future studies of fleas and roaches. Now Dr. Cruz studies ways to live side by side with the creatures that share our planet. He was recently awarded a presidential medal for his efforts to keep deadly pesticides out of the home.

Humberto Cruz

PETS REALLY LOVE THE PET GUY

QUESTIONS EVERYWHERE Questions are just signs that you are curious. What happens when a spider's web gets damaged? How can you keep mice out of the house? Why do cats wag their tails? Why do dogs wag their tails? Questions are often the door to scientific discoveries. Experiments grow from questions. Once you get started exploring, who knows where you'll end up? Enjoy your questions and let them send you on a scientific journey!

Here are some questions from kids at El Portal Elementary School in California:

- ▶ How much will my pet shark eat?
- ▶ Are dogs colorblind?
- ▶ Why do most cats hate water?
- ▶ Why do cats push up their hair when they are scared?
- ▶ Will one parakeet teach another one to be tame?
- ▶ Why do cats lick their butts, but they don't get sick?
- ▶ Do dogs run faster before or after they eat?
- ▶ How will my pet bird react to shiny things?
- ▶ How old do guinea pigs get?
- ▶ How do fish have babies?
- ▶ Do rabbits like to eat pizza?
- ▶ How often does my cat eat?
- ▶ Will a dog play with a cat?
- ▶ Can a spider climb a wall with soap on it?
- ▶ How does my dog react to a flashlight?

WHAT IF . . .

When you follow your questions, they lead to tests. What if I fed my dog some cat food? Would it eat it? What if I put a cricket in a box? Would it sing? As you wonder about the animals that share your home, you might be able to turn some of these wonderings into tests. Here are some guidelines for tests:

- ▶ Use fair tests. (For example: if you were testing to see if one breed of dog can retrieve balls better than another breed, you would want to use the same type of ball. It wouldn't be fair to throw a basketball to a toy poodle and a tennis ball to a Great Dane.)

► Treat animals humanely. All animals, whether they are your pet cats or a visiting house cricket, should be treated with respect. That means that whatever you do, **do not** harm them in any way.

► Perform your test several times to see if the same thing happens every time.

► Record what happens by taking notes, pictures, or video footage.

► Share your results with friends and family, and challenge them to repeat your test to see if they get the same results.

THE SCIENTIFIC METHOD

The scientific method is like a guide to discovery. As you investigate the creatures in your house, use the following process and see what happens!

1. **Start with a question or guess.** (For example: Which kind of birdseed is my parakeet's favorite?) Write it down. Keep a lab notebook.

2. **Test.** (For example: Offer your parakeet three different types of seeds on a plate. Watch to see which seeds he eats the most.) Record your results.

3. **Repeat, repeat, repeat!** Do your test several times under the same conditions to see if the same things happen. This way you will know if your results happened by chance or not. Write down what happens each time so you can compare.

4. **Make conclusions.** Why do you think you got the results you did? Jot down your ideas.

5. **Modify and retest.** If you feel like it, you can change the test slightly and do it over. (For example: Turn the plate of seeds to make sure your parakeet isn't just eating the seeds closest to him.)

The great thing about experiments is that whether they reward you with the answer you were seeking or not, you always end up with something, even if it's another mystery.

HAMSTERS, GERBILS, AND TWEETY BIRD

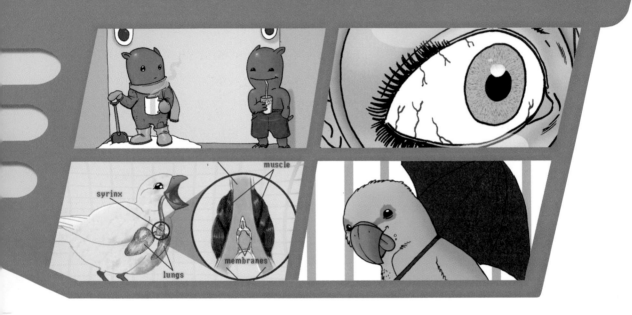

When people make homes, they try to keep out not only the rain and cold but also other animals. Inside these exclusive shelters, however, it can become lonely. For centuries people have brought creatures into their homes. Whether they keep parakeets and gerbils in cages or goldfish in bowls, these animal housemates provide hours of entertainment. Whether you have a pet boa constrictor or a tame rabbit, you can keep yourself busy by watching them carefully.

HOW TO BE AN ANIMAL DETECTIVE

binoculars	tape recorder
magnifying lens	video camera
notebook	Polaroid camera

Some folks think animals are more exciting to watch than TV. Find out for yourself! Pretend you are a spy and keep track of the actions of your housemates. Choose a comfortable place to watch your pet and take notes on the animal's actions.

Write down what you see and any questions that you have, such as, "Why does my bird stop singing in the dark?" or "Does my hamster play with more energy before or after she eats?"

11

BIRDSONGS Male birds sing to attract females or to tell other males to stay away. Some birds, such as canaries, sing a variety of different tunes. The older the male canary, the more different songs he sings. How does all this singing affect the canaries who are the intended audience? German and Japanese researchers played tapes of male songsters to caged females. They discovered that the larger the variety of songs played, the faster the females built nests. They also laid eggs sooner and laid more eggs per nest than females exposed to a smaller variety of songs. Older male canaries are usually better partners because they provide more food for the young nestlings. Do more tunes send a signal to the female that she can have a bigger family because she'll have an older, more helpful mate?

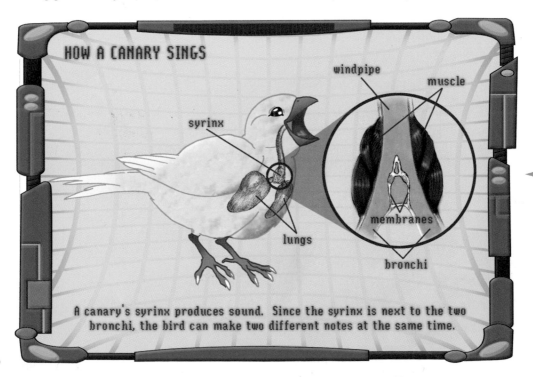

HOW A CANARY SINGS

windpipe

muscle

syrinx

lungs

membranes

bronchi

A canary's syrinx produces sound. Since the syrinx is next to the two bronchi, the bird can make two different notes at the same time.

CHELAN'S SHOWER Alison had noticed birds washing themselves in puddles and birdbaths many times. She thought that her pet parakeet, Chelan, would enjoy a shower from a spray bottle and would try to wash in it. Using a spray bottle, Alison sprayed Chelan three times. Here are her results:

test 1 Chelan closed her eyes and spread her feathers to dry.

test 2 She closed her eyes and turned her back to the spray.

test 3 She just closed her eyes.

Alison decided that her hypothesis was incorrect because Chelan didn't take a bath in the water spray. In fact, she decided that her bird didn't like the spray at all. Do you agree?

TOASTY PUPS Young hamsters are born almost helpless. With legs splayed out to the side, they look more like penguins than the scurrying hamsters they will grow up to be. They snuggle up to their mothers for warmth. They drink her milk until they are big enough to explore. For several years, Christiana Leonard studied hamster pups. In her lab at the University of Florida, she watched newborn pups and tried some simple experiments.

Soon after birth, the pups still have their eyes closed. But Christiana found out that they could find their way to the nest when removed. Using their front legs like oars, they immediately started "rowing" toward the nest. On reaching the nest, the pups rooted around in the crowd of brothers and sisters until they reached the middle where it is warmest. Was it the heat that attracted them?

To test this question, Christiana placed very young pups in a special box that was cool at one end and warm at the other. Without hesitating, the pups went to the warm end. When placed on a cool spot, the pups always moved toward warmth. When set on a warm spot, they stayed put!

If your hamster has pups, try a variation of the experiment. Gently place the pups 10 to 20 centimeters apart. Do you think they will move toward each other and huddle to get warm and cozy?

Many of us share our homes with cats and dogs, but do we really know them? Often we label their behaviors as if these creatures were fellow humans. Though we get close to pet dogs and cats, it's important to remember that they sense the world differently than we do. Dogs use their ears, which can hear much better than ours, to listen to sounds we can't even hear. By watching them, we can better understand how they respond to their surroundings and live their lives.

DOG BEHAVIOR

Pet owners and scientists often interpret dog behavior differently. Scientists watch dogs in wild packs. They base their ideas on certain behaviors—such as tail wagging or licking—on how the dogs relate to each other. Pet owners may base their ideas on assumptions that dogs think like people.

Watch how dogs behave with other dogs and with people. Perhaps you can decide for yourself what their behaviors mean.

BEHAVIOR	PET OWNER THINKS	SCIENTIST THINKS
Jumping	Poorly trained	Showing who is in charge
Tail wagging	Show of love	Greeting
Licking	Show of love	Greeting, identifying each other, grooming

When two dogs meet, the dominant dog stands up straight, with ears and tail up. The submissive dog stays lower with its tail held down.

CAT BEHAVIOR

What is your cat's favorite scratching spot? Cats scratch table legs, chairs, and other places to remove old, worn claw sheaths and reveal new, sharp ones. Check their scratching spots and you may discover what look like broken claws. These are just old claw coverings.

Cats also scratch to leave their scent. On the pads of their feet are special scent-making glands. Favorite places to leave scent are places where other cats or humans in their family have left their scent, such as couches or chairs. Scratching is also just plain exercise. After all, cats need to keep in good shape.

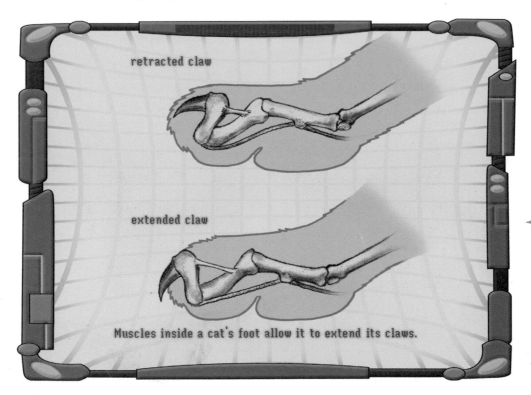

retracted claw

extended claw

Muscles inside a cat's foot allow it to extend its claws.

ZOO Fieldwork

CAT WATCH Rachel has two cats, Fig and Tom. She watched each of them and made notes on what she observed.

TOM:
- Tom seems to have a taste for bugs.
- He likes to sleep most of the time.
- He is easily spooked.
- Eat, eat, eat! He goes through a whole bag of food in a week.
- Question: Why does he eat bugs?

FIG:
- Fig is very frisky. He plays with Tom a lot.
- He lies in the sink for ten minutes a day. He seems to love water.
- Question: Why does he sleep in the sink?

As you can see from Rachel's notes, the cats acted quite differently. What do their behaviors tell you about these cats? What are you basing your conclusions on?

CATS AND SOUND Does your cat leave the room when you practice the clarinet? Does it perk up its ears when it hears a can of food being opened? Brittany was curious about how her cats would react to different sounds. When she turned on the microwave, they showed no reaction. When she played the piano, they showed no reaction. Did they like these sounds? When Brittany opened and closed the door, the cats perked up their ears. She thought they were afraid. When she played her flute, they seemed afraid again. She concluded that they didn't like the door or flute sounds, but liked the other sounds. Which sounds do your pets like or dislike?

AMAZING CAT FACTS
- The average territory size for a cat living in the wild is 175 acres. City cats may roam over only ⅕ of an acre.

- The champion mouser of all times was a cat from Lancashire, England. It killed more than 22,000 mice in its 23-year life! Another British kitty caught 12,480 rats in just 6 years.

- The oldest recorded age of a domestic cat is 36 years.

NOTES ON SARGENT Rico paid close attention to his young dog Sargent. He recorded his observations of Sarge's behavior. As you can see by Rico's notes, scientists can record a lot of information without having to worry about writing complete sentences.

After keeping notes on Sargent, Rico concluded that his dog is very active. He wondered if all young dogs are like that. He also concluded that some of Sarge's behaviors were reactions to Rico's behavior. Do you have any ideas why Sarge behaved as he did? How would you search for the answers to your questions?

RICO'S NOTES

- sniffs box
- drags his bed with teeth
- I say, "Sarge"—he runs up stairs
- pushes me around
- runs down stairs and fights with his cover
- lies down
- I go pet him—he rolls over and fights with cover
- starts biting my pants
- goes and wrestles cover
- bites my pants again
- lies down
- I run across garage—he runs after me
- runs to bed
- runs up stairs
- bites my pants
- walks down stairs
- sniffs garage floor
- sniffs Tonka truck
- bites cover

CHOICE MEALS Does your pet have a favorite food? Would you be able to predict what it might choose from a tasty array of treats? Nicole set out three dishes. One contained a dog snack, another contained lettuce, and the third contained sausage. She thought that her dog would prefer the doggie snack. After she had set the snacks out, she brought her dog in from another room. Then she jotted down his dining behavior. In three tests, her dog munched the sausage first and the doggie snacks second. The lettuce was left alone. What did you think her dog would choose? Nicole thought her dog preferred the sausage because it was tastier.

AMAZING DOG FACTS

- Most large pet dogs can reach speeds of 30 kilometers per hour, while pet greyhounds can zoom up to 70 kilometers per hour.

- According to some estimates, a dog's sense of smell may be one million times greater than a human's sense of smell.

- All dogs, including your Fido or Fifi, are direct descendants of wolves.

- The oldest recorded age of a dog is 29 years and 5 months.

- The smallest dog in history was a Yorkshire terrier that was about the size of a mouse.

DOGS AND BALLS Veterinarian Myrna Milani had a cocker spaniel patient that was always calm when she had a ball in her mouth. Myrna could take the dog's temperature and examine her without worrying about her leaping off of the examination table. As long as she held the ball, she was cooperative.

Later on Myrna met a mail carrier who was almost attacked by a cocker spaniel that had bitten him on previous occasions. In self-defense, the mail carrier picked up a ball from the yard and threw it at the dog to scare it off. Instead, the dog chased the ball, retrieved it, and dropped it at the mail carrier's feet, wanting to play some more! From then on, the mail carrier always carried a ball with him to toss to dogs so they would play rather than attack him.

Have you noticed any interesting behavior with dogs and toys? Can you think of some experiments to do with them?

Many creatures that sneak under doors or through windows to seek shelter in our homes cause no harm. In stories they actually are quite helpful. Where would Pinocchio be without Jiminy Cricket? Where would Wilbur the pig be without his spider friend Charlotte? Crickets, ladybugs, spiders, and many other small visitors to our houses can provide good company and entertainment if we watch them carefully.

Are your uninvited guests active throughout the day and night? Do crickets sing at certain times? What time of day do you see centipedes? What time of year do you notice ladybugs indoors? Keep tabs on the activities and presence of your little visitors. Maybe you can determine if they are diurnal (active in the day) or nocturnal (creatures of the night). How do the nocturnal creatures react to light?

SPIDER BEHAVIOR Cobweb spiders are commonly found indoors and are often called house spiders. They hang upside down from irregular mazelike webs that become cobwebs when abandoned. Though these webs are annoying to housecleaners, these spiders are excellent hunters of household pests.

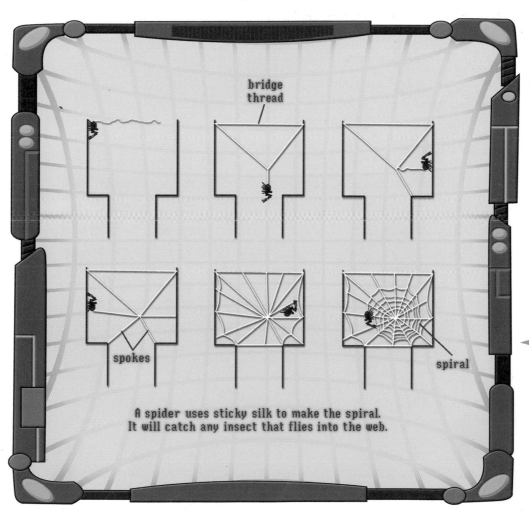

A spider uses sticky silk to make the spiral.
It will catch any insect that flies into the web.

UNINVITED GUESTS

CRICKET: Field and house crickets will make themselves at home inside houses. They eat a wide variety of foods, including dry cat and dog food. Natives of Europe, house crickets have been introduced to other parts of the world, including North America.

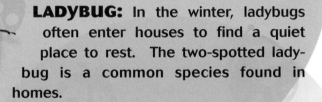

LADYBUG: In the winter, ladybugs often enter houses to find a quiet place to rest. The two-spotted ladybug is a common species found in homes.

CENTIPEDE: These many-legged critters wander into homes and hunt any insects they can find. They have poison jaws that paralyze the insects they eat. When disturbed, they will sting, but the small ones found in your house won't hurt you.

MOTH FLY: These small, hairy, moth-like flies hold their wings over their backs like a roof. They munch on decaying matter and sometimes are found hanging out near sink drains.

ROLYPOLY: Also known as wood lice or pill bugs, these small terrestrial bugs munch fruit and decaying matter. Sometimes they wander indoors from backyard gardens.

SPIDER: There are many species of spiders that live in houses. Some, like wolf or jumping spiders, roam freely and pounce on flies and other prey. Those that build webs indoors include funnel web spiders and daddy longlegs. Few spiders bite humans. Most bites blamed on them are actually from other small creatures. Spiders are helpful in controlling indoor pests, such as houseflies and mosquitoes.

ZOO Fieldwork

LOST VISITORS? Have you ever found a bug wandering around your house? Is it on a particular mission? Or is it just lost? Rolypolies sometimes crawl indoors. Elijio caught a rolypoly. He wondered if it would always walk in a different direction each time it was released from the container he had caught it in. On a sheet of paper, he drew a circle about 20 centimeters in diameter. Inside this, he drew a smaller circle about 6 centimeters in diameter. He released the rolypoly in the middle and traced its path with a pencil. After repeating this 20 times, Elijio found that the circle was covered with lines leading in all directions. He repeated this with another rolypoly and got the same results. He decided that rolypolies just want to leave, and it doesn't matter to them which way they go. Do you think that some of the bugs that visit your home are simply lost?

LIGHT REACTIONS A flashlight beam in the eye is annoying to people. Does a flashlight beam annoy spiders? Nick thought that spiders would not like a small beam pointed at them. He set up a test to find out how they would react. He turned off the lights in his bedroom and then used three different-sized flashlights to beam in on three different spiders that lived in the nooks and crannies of his room. After each flash, he jotted down notes. The results surprised him. None of the spiders reacted in any way to any of the lights. Were the spiders just used to his bedroom lights going off and on all the time? Nick wondered if spiders just don't care about flashlights or science experiments!

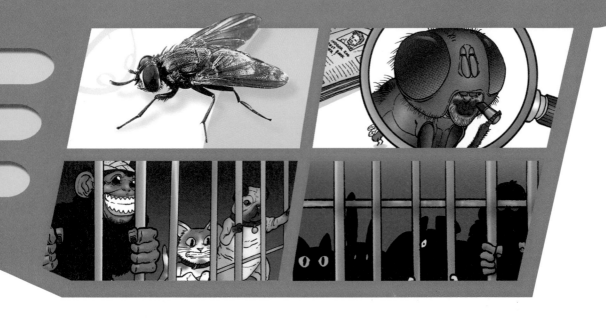

No matter how clean you keep your home, unwanted pests will most likely appear. Many creatures arrive at a particular season. Some species of ants will enter homes after the first good rain of the spring. Flies become abundant in summer, when there is lots of stinky garbage to breed in. Evicting these trespassing visitors has been a test of human cleverness for centuries.

Have you ever watched a housefly do a somersault and land on the ceiling? How do you think ants react to strange, smelly substances? Though these animals can be very pesky, observing them can be more entertaining than a rerun on TV.

HOW TO MAKE A FLYTRAP

SUPPLIES

3 1-liter-sized plastic bottles	duct tape
125 milliliters acrylic house paint	4 rubber bands
knife (use only with supervision of adult)	bait

1. Slightly dilute the paint and pour it into one bottle. Turn the bottle to coat the lower ⅔ of the bottle with paint.

2. After the paint has dried, ask an adult to help you cut a small door on either side of the bottle.

3. Cut the bottom off the second bottle and cut flaps along the bottom edge.

4. Cut the top and bottom off the third bottle and cut out a rectangular section of the wall about 20 centimeters long and 10 centimeters wide. Cut a flap along one of the narrow ends and roll into a tube. Hold the tube in place with rubber bands.

5. Place the tube on top of the threaded opening of the painted bottle. Attach tightly with duct tape. Use another piece of tape to close the top of the tube so that only a small opening is left that is big enough for a fly to go through.

6. Place the bottomless bottle over the other bottle and tube. Secure it around the base with tape.

7. Set the trap, with bait, in a fly-infested part of your house. You can try using various bits of smelly trash for bait. Or combine one package dry yeast, 60 milliliters water, and 5 milliliters sugar for bait. Release captured flies outdoors.

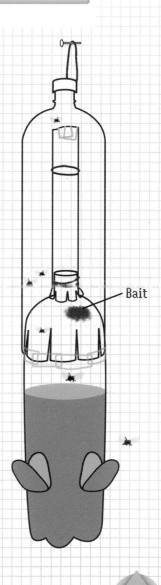

Bait

31

GALLERY OF UNWANTED PESTS

ANT: All ants except those with wings are female workers that cannot lay eggs. Ants live in colonies, and the workers forage for food. Some types of ants prefer sweets, others seeds, meat, or wood. When disturbed, ants often produce a smelly substance called formic acid. Formic acid acts like an alarm to warn other ants of danger. Many of the ant species that invade houses are non-natives that have adapted to human communities.

BOOK LOUSE: An insect found in dusty cracks and corners, including the pages of books. Book lice feed mostly on molds.

CLOTHES MOTH: This straw-colored moth, about the size of a ladybug, lays its eggs on wool, silk, and other fibers. The tiny caterpillar eats the cloth and makes a cocoon out of fragments of its food.

COCKROACH: A relative of grasshoppers and crickets that feeds on a wide variety of foods. Cockroaches found in homes are usually tropical species, such as the oriental cockroach, which have adapted to indoor life. Most have an odor, but they are not carriers of specific diseases.

FRUIT FLY: A tiny fly that often has spotted wings. Many species lay their eggs in fruit such as cherries or apples.

HOUSEFLY: The most common fly found in people's homes. Houseflies lay eggs in garbage, manure, and other decaying matter. The eggs hatch into maggots. An adult housefly does not bite. Instead, it uses its spongelike mouth to sop up food. Flies can spread serious diseases such as typhoid fever and dysentery. The stable fly looks like a housefly, but it bites.

MEALWORM: The larva of a beetle that feeds on seeds and flours. The brown or black adults have hard outer wings, like other beetles, and are the size of a rice grain.

MOUSE: The house mouse is the most common species found in homes. House mice depend upon human food, such as grains or cereals. They don't need access to fresh water and can survive on 3 milliliters of food a day. Mice also gnaw at books, clothing, wood, and other materials to get stuffing for nests. They can spread disease by contaminating food or utensils with their droppings.

SILVERFISH: A wingless insect that lives inside houses. Silverfish munch on the starch in old books, starch paste in old wallpaper, and cloth. They prefer damp places.

WHITEFLY: An insect of the tropics that survives well in houses and greenhouses. Whiteflies suck sap from leaves and often cause serious damage to houseplants.

ZOOFieldwork

MOUTH PRINTS Other folks might consider flies totally worthless. But as a fly spy, Brianna found them to be an excellent laboratory animal.

To observe the use of fly tongues (proboscises), Brianna mixed some sugar, water, and food coloring. She brushed the mixture onto a sheet of paper and set the paper in the middle of a larger sheet of newspaper. In a few minutes, a fly discovered the sweet paper. After the fly sopped up the mixture, Brianna checked out the prints that were left on the surrounding newsprint. What do you think the prints looked like?

AMAZING FLY FACTS

fast flap: can beat wings over 200 times per second

rapid transit: can fly up to 40 kilometers per hour

sensational talent: can taste with leg hairs

love stinks: Females attract males with an irresistible odor called a pheromone.

time flies: Mother lays several hundred eggs at a time, which hatch in eight to twelve hours into legless maggots. In one to three weeks, maggots transform into pupae from which emerge adult flies ready to mate and lay more eggs.

live hard, die fast: Most flies live an average of only a few days. If all her offspring and their offspring survived, within five months there could be as many as 5,598,720,000,000 flies from one mama fly.

SLOBBERED SNACKS One famous entomologist, Vincent Dethier, spent years in the mid-1900s experimenting with flies. He conducted tests to discover how they use hairs to taste and what foods females prefer when their eggs are developing. In another test, he discovered that blowflies prefer food that has already been slobbered on by other blowflies.

Do houseflies prefer slobbered food too? Repeat Vincent's experiment (below) and see if you get the same results.

1. Cook 250 milliliters of oatmeal or cornmeal. Stir in 62 milliliters of milk and spread a thick layer on the surface of three small plates.
2. Tightly cover one half of each plate with a piece of aluminum foil.
3. Place all three plates in a fly-infested place. Wait until several flies begin dining on each plate, let them eat for a few minutes, then shoo them away.
4. Remove the foil and spin the plates 180 degrees so that slobbered food is on the opposite side.
5. Wait for the flies to return. Do they prefer one side to the other?

LAB TORTURE

For years scientists have kept lab animals for research. Monkeys, rabbits, cats, and rats are all used for medical experiments. They are infected with diseases, poisoned, operated on, and poked and probed in many ways. Not everyone agrees that animals should be used in this way. Many people think it is cruel to use animals for lab tests. Research scientists argue that the use of animals for research saves both human and animal lives as cures are found for diseases and other medical problems.

Few people, however, complain when exterminators kill cockroaches, flies, or other household pests. One of the reasons that Vincent Dethier chose to use blowflies as lab animals was because

they were inexpensive to breed and raise. But he also picked them because no one would object to his experimenting with them. There are no organizations to prevent cruelty to household pests. Should there be one? Is it OK to mistreat one animal and not another? Even though animals that we consider pests are not well liked, perhaps we can still show them respect as living creatures. As a scientist, you can decide to make your research cruelty free.

Hidden from sight in all parts of our homes and even inside our bodies are minute organisms called bacteria. Bacteria are neither plants nor animals, although some move about like microscopic creatures. Molds are a type of fungus that are also uninvited guests in our homes. Bacteria, molds, and the tiny larvae of insects are all found on food that has become a bit old. Though they can damage stored food, they also help us get rid of food waste.

If you don't eat your food, somebody else will. Hungry molds feed on the starches and sugars of lunches left in desks. Tiny beetles munch dry old crackers left too long in the cupboard. These creatures contribute to the process of decomposition, recycling old food by breaking it apart.

HOW TO MAKE COMPOST

Have you ever thought of what goes into your kitchen garbage can? A lot of the things we throw away can be recycled, especially the discarded parts of plants. Banana peels, apple cores, onion skins, leftover rice, and any other things that come from plants can be turned into useful topsoil for a garden through a process called composting. To make compost, all you need is a little out-door space. You can use one corner of your yard. If you live in an apartment, ask your teacher if you can make a compost pile at school, or check with local community gardens.

COMPOST TIPS

- Keep your pile from getting soggy. A soggy pile will begin to stink like a manure heap. Once a pile becomes soggy, mixing in dried leaves or straw can dry it out.

- Do not add meat or dairy products to the compost. These can attract rats and other pests that you probably don't want in your backyard or schoolyard.

1. At your chosen compost spot, mix equal parts of kitchen waste and dead leaves or straw.
2. Add a shovelful of garden soil and enough water to make the pile moist but not soggy.
3. Add more kitchen waste and leaves or grass clippings each week. Turn the whole pile with a shovel each time you add something.
4. Check out the little critters, such as worms and other living things, that have made their home in your compost!
5. After a few months, dig out the older compost. Add it to your garden.

DECOMPOSITION Everything eventually falls apart. Giant trees and old peanut butter sandwiches break down into smaller particles and become part of the soil. This process of breaking down is called decomposition. Fungi, insects, bacteria, and other living things are all part of this process of munching up leftovers. For example, worms eat leaves shed by trees. Their castings (poop) are basically soil.

Bacteria are important decomposers. Some types of bacteria need a lot of air to survive. Other kinds of bacteria can decompose materials in airless places like bogs and swamps, but they create a stinky gas as they feed. These are the bacteria that cause garbage to get really nasty smelling.

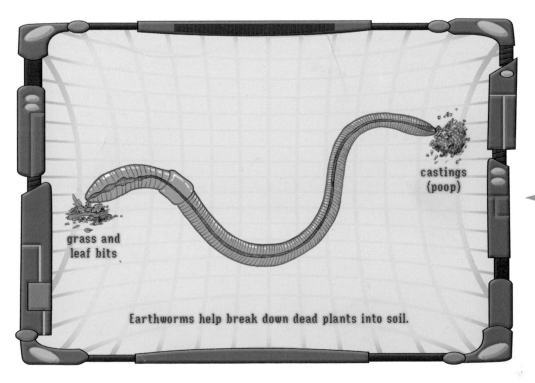

castings
(poop)

grass and
leaf bits

Earthworms help break down dead plants into soil.

ZOO Fieldwork

LIVELY MUSH Spencer wanted to see if he could make mold and grass grow on bread. After soaking the bread, he dropped it in a plastic bag and stored it in a classroom cubbyhole. When he checked a few days later he discovered it was gone. The janitor had tossed it out, thinking it was trash. He repeated the test and put the bag in a cubbyhole. Once more it disappeared. For a third time, Spencer soaked some bread and stored it in a bag. To keep it safe, he crammed it way in the back of a cubbyhole. It was still there two weeks later when he checked it.

Instead of mold or grass, the bag was full of a brown mush and hundreds of fruit flies. Their pupal cases were all over the inside of the bag. Spencer thought the whole thing smelled like mildew. He believed that if he had added dirt, then grass and mold would have grown instead of flies.

What do you think? Try his test and see what happens, but do it someplace where the stinky smells and possible fruit fly swarms won't get you in trouble.

PEOPLE EATERS

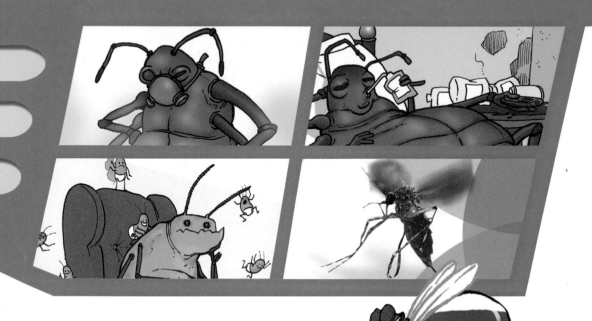

Though most animals enter human homes to eat people's food or materials, there are some that seek fresh blood. These bloodsuckers may enter the house on the bodies of pet cats or dogs that have been roaming the neighborhood, or on the heads of kids who have been at school. Once settled in our cozy nests, these animals have a constant food supply.

PEOPLE AND PET EATERS

BEDBUG: This belongs to a group of insects called true bugs. It has a flattened body and beaklike mouthparts. Unlike most other true bugs, it is wingless. Bedbugs feed on birds and mammals at night. They hide in crevices during the day. Though rare in most homes in the United States, bedbugs still thrive in many parts of the world.

FLEA: This insect has a flattened body and needlelike mouthparts used for sucking blood. Fleas have no wings, but they are excellent jumpers. Fleas that munch on people also eat the blood of other animals, such as cats or dogs. Eggs are laid on the host or in the host's nest.

MOSQUITO: Its name is Spanish for "small fly." As a larva, it lives in water. It emerges as a winged adult. Only females feed on blood. The males, which have brushlike antennae, sip nectar from flowers and drink other plant juices. Some species of adult mosquitoes will hibernate over the winter, sometimes in houses.

SUCKING LOUSE: The crab, head, and body lice are the only lice that feed on humans. The head louse is the most common. It clings to the scalp or hairs with claws and hooks on its mouth. Eggs are attached to hairs and hatch after a week. Regular bathing and clothes washing help prevent lice outbreaks.

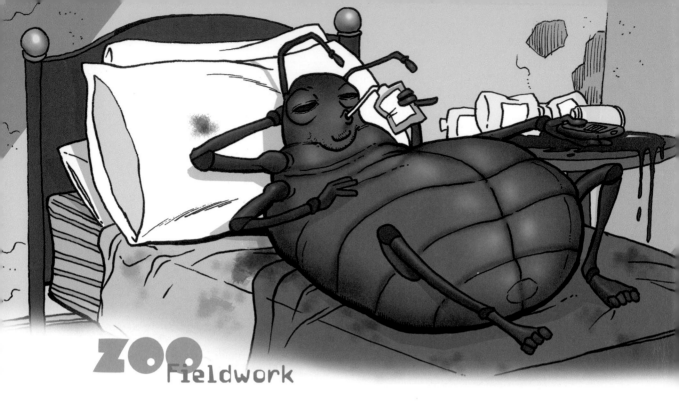

ZOO Fieldwork

DEDICATED SCIENCE How far will you go to satisfy your curiosity? If you wanted to learn more about how mosquitoes get a meal, would you let a horde of them dine on your blood? Robert Usinger, an entomologist from California, spent many years studying bedbugs. These little insects were once very common bedmates for most folks. In order to grow, bedbugs must feed on blood until they are bloated like small balloons.

In his lab, Robert fed the bugs by attaching their cages to rabbits. When he had to take his bedbugs to scientific meetings, he fed them by strapping the cage to his own arm! Not only did Robert have to put up with their diet, he had to withstand their body odor. Bedbugs stink! They are related to stinkbugs, and this stink seems to help them survive.

Bats, which are a common host of bedbugs, will eat mealworms like most kids eat candy. When mealworms are smeared with the scent of bedbugs, however, bats refuse to dine.

FLEA FAMILIES When raising a large family, it helps to have plenty of food for all the growing youngsters. Miriam Rothschild, one of the world's foremost flea experts, discovered rabbit fleas won't even mate until they have a sure sign of food in the future. When bunnies get ready to mate, their ears get hotter. This signals the fleas to camp out on them. Ten days before the rabbit doe gives birth, hormones in her blood cause the fleas to get ready to mate. Shortly before the little bunnies are born, the fleas head down to find the nest and newborns. They are just in time. They mate and lay eggs that hatch little fleas ready to feed in this nest full of baby bunnies with fresh blood.

AMAZING FLEA FACTS

forceful leaps: A flea blasts off at 140 times the force of gravity as many as 600 times an hour.

high jump: 25 centimeters

longest wait between meals: Antarctic fleas go hungry for up to nine months each year.

favorite foods: Rodents, such as mice and rats, are preferred by three out of four flea species.

weirdest flea exterminator: a miniature cannon devised by Queen Charlotte of Sweden

Miriam wondered if folktales about fleas liking women more than men are based on the attraction of fleas to human sex hormones. Do women in your family get bitten more than the men do?

CONTROLLING FLEAS

"Sleep tight and don't let the bedbugs bite. If they do, hit them with a shoe until they are black and blue."

In the past, blood-sucking vermin were tougher to control than they are today. Only the wealthy could afford to employ hardworking exterminators who crawled around rooms seeking out each pest so they could whack them with a shoe or some other weapon. With the invention of pesticides, the number of people eaters in homes has decreased, but many pests are becoming resistant to these poisons. Though bedbugs and lice are now uncommon in many homes throughout the world, fleas continue to be a constant problem.

Controlling fleas is a big business. All sorts of pesticides are used in killing fleas, but many pet owners worry about these poisons harming their pets. One way to reduce the flea population in your home without resorting to toxic substances is to use substances that kill flea larvae by drying them out. Minute crystals called DE (diatomaceous earth) actually make holes in the skin of little insects such as ants and fleas, causing them to lose precious fluids. Other powders, such as boric acid, kill fleas by poisoning their stomachs. Neither is harmful to humans or pets unless breathed in during application to floors and carpets. Use a dust respirator when applying any powder and always work under the supervision of an adult!

Glossary

diurnal: active by day

dysentery: a painful inflammation of the large intestine

entomologist: a scientist who studies insects

hormone: an internal substance produced by the body that regulates certain bodily functions

larvae: insects in an early stage of growth

maggots: the legless larvae of some insects, such as flies

native: originating in a particular region

nocturnal: active at night

pheromone: a substance produced by an animal that makes other animals of the same species respond in a certain way

pupae: insects in a growth stage just before adulthood

species: a group of animals or plants with common traits

territory: the area that an animal claims for its use

Metric Conversion Table

When you know:	Multiply by:	To find:
centimeters (cm)	0.394	inches (in.)
meters (m)	3.281	feet (ft.)
kilometers per hour (km/h)	0.621	miles per hour (mph)
hectares (ha)	2.471	acres
milliliters (ml)	0.2	teaspoons (tsp.)
milliliters (ml)	0.004	cups (c.)
liters (l)	1.057	quarts (qt.)
grams (g)	0.035	ounces (oz.)

To convert degrees Celsius (°C) to degrees Fahrenheit (°F), multiply by 9 and divide by 5, then add 32.

Index

Photo Acknowledgments
The photographs have been reproduced with the permission of: © Dwight R. Kuhn, pp. 2, 24, 26 (millipede), 27 (spider), 33 (mouse), 42, 43 (flea, mosquito); © Robert and Linda Mitchell, pp. 26 (cricket, ladybug), 27 (moth fly, rolypoly), 30, 32, 33 (housefly, mealworm, silverfish, whitefly), 43 (sucking louse).